Jealousy is Not for Me

A Guide for Freeing Yourself from Envy

Written by Molly Wigand
Illustrated by R.W. Alley

ONE
CARING
PLACE

Abbey Press
St. Meinrad, IN 47577

For the dedicated teachers
at Mill Creek Elementary,
who helped my kids in a million ways.

Text © 2007 Molly Wigand
Illustrations © 2007 Saint Meinrad Archabbey
Published by One Caring Place
Abbey Press
St. Meinrad, Indiana 47577

Library of Congress Catalog Number
2007933905

ISBN 978-0-87029-408-2

Printed in the United States of America

A Message to Parents, Teachers, and Other Caring Adults

Our goal as adult caregivers is to empower children to become happy, safe, good people. In a society that breeds materialism and encourages constant competition, freeing children from jealousy and envy is a daunting challenge.

Media messages urge children to get the newest, fanciest, most expensive, and stylish things. Children learn that to be "cool kids," they must have the "best" of everything, from cell phones to sporting equipment to video games to designer clothing.

Competition in school and sports, too, makes kids feel envious of friends and teammates. "Doing your best" doesn't feel like enough, as kids compete for spots on elite teams or admission to exclusive schools. Kids begin to measure their achievements against the success of others. The resulting jealousy takes the joy and fun out of participating in sports and makes it difficult for kids to be friends.

In busy families and classrooms, it often feels impossible to devote the same energy and focus to every child. Special needs and high-achieving children may garner more attention than others. It's natural for kids "in the middle" to envy those who may dominate the spotlight.

We can help children process these human inequities and the jealous feelings they foster. By teaching children to be content with what they have and proud of who they are, we minimize competition and jealousy. When the "green-eyed monster" appears, we can help our children verbalize their emotions, so they can move beyond envy to contentment and joy.

Of course, the best way to teach this or any lesson to a child is to model the behaviors and attitudes we are teaching. Do we really need the newest cars, biggest houses, and most prestigious jobs? What can we do to demonstrate the joy of sharing our blessings with others? Are we committed to giving our love and attention equally to the children in our lives?

As mindful adults, we can make our homes, schools, and communities places of contentment, where hearts are free of jealousy and we all appreciate our blessings every day.

—Molly Wigand

What Is Jealousy?

Growing up means learning to deal with many different feelings. Sometimes feelings are happy…like being thankful or excited or friendly. But some feelings are harder to deal with…like being sad or afraid or lonely.

Jealousy is a hard feeling. When we're jealous, we wish we could take the good stuff someone else has. We might become jealous of other people's stuff, like toys or cars or computer games. Sometimes we get jealous of the attention other people receive. Or we may be jealous of what someone else can do.

Whatever the cause of our jealousy, it can make us feel angry or sad or afraid.

Jealousy—It's Only Human!

Little kids, big kids, teenagers, moms and dads, teachers, grandmas and grandpas… everyone feels jealous from time to time. It's a normal part of being human. And once we learn more about jealousy, we can learn to handle it and be a little happier every day.

Jealousy has been around for a long time. It's even in the Bible, where one of the Ten Commandments asks us not to be jealous. Five hundred years ago, the famous writer Shakespeare called jealousy "the green-eyed monster."

Wants or Needs?

Have you ever felt jealous of the cool stuff a friend has? Maybe your friend has a brand-new bike that's faster than yours. Maybe your cousin has the latest video game system. Maybe you wish you had these things instead!

When this happens, we can try to think about the difference between what we *want* and what we *need*. Television commercials make people *want* to have the best of everything. But when we think about the things we actually *need* to be happy people, we realize God is taking pretty good care of us.

Jealous Brothers, Jealous Sisters

Sometimes jealousy can happen in your own family. When a new baby arrives, you might be afraid about how this will change your life. It's normal to feel this way.

Brothers and sisters may have other reasons to feel jealous, too. Maybe your sister is a soccer star with lots of trophies. Or maybe your brother is sick and gets extra presents and attention.

When you feel jealous at home, talk to your mom or dad. They will tell you that no matter what happens in your family, you're an important person who is loved very much.

Competing in the Classroom

Do you ever feel jealous at school? It can hurt when you try your best to get a good grade and someone else does better on a test. Remember that every person has special talents, and your turn to shine is sure to come.

We all want teachers to like us. Most teachers try not to play favorites, but maybe it seems like somebody is the "teacher's pet." If you feel neglected, talk to your parent or another trusted grown-up about it.

You'll learn that doing your best and being yourself makes you feel less jealous. The ups and downs of school will be easier to take.

Life Isn't a Contest!

Comparing yourself to other kids can make jealousy pop up quickly. To avoid this, many athletes follow the old saying, "Run your own race." Whatever you're doing, focus on your own effort and goals. Don't worry about who's faster or slower or who gets the highest or lowest grade. Life isn't a contest, and everyone has a chance to do well.

Think of all the special qualities you have. Start with things you're good at, like sports or music or spelling. Then consider the "inside things," like kindness and patience and being a good friend.

Best Friends Forever?

How do you feel when your best friend gets a new friend? Probably sad and angry, and maybe a little jealous. You may wish that the new friend would go away or find a different friend.

It's important to talk to your friend about how this makes you feel. You can also use this as a chance to make a new friend. Maybe someone else is feeling left out, too.

Being jealous can sometimes make a friend want some space away from you. Remember that people don't own each other, and everyone is free to be friends with other people. There's plenty of friendship to go around!

When Friends Are Jealous of You

It's not fun when you feel jealous, and it's also not fun when people feel jealous of you. If a friend starts acting funny when you have your turn in the spotlight, remember that jealousy is normal for everybody.

Help the friend understand what you've learned…that we all have different talents and different ways to shine. Maybe you can help the friend see the ways he or she is a very special person. We all like to hear that once in awhile!

What's Up with Braggers?

Some people are braggers who actually like other people to be jealous of them. They may brag about getting new toys or cards or a fancy new house.

Believe it or not, people who brag like this often don't feel good about themselves. They think that bragging makes them better people. You can try to tell people how their bragging makes you feel. But if they keep bragging, and it keeps making you feel bad, you don't have to listen.

Don't Hide It Inside!

Jealousy gets worse when we hold it inside. Practice talking about your feelings, first at home, and then with friends.

If you're jealous of a friend at school, try saying, "I feel jealous when you always win the spelling bee." Maybe that friend will help you. And maybe that friend will tell you about a time he or she felt jealous, too. Sharing those feelings "clears the air" so you can be friends without jealousy getting in the way.

Remember, saying "I feel…" is a good way to help people understand. (Much better than saying, "Why do you ALWAYS have to win the spelling bee?")

Feeling Thankful Really Helps!

Whether at home or school or hanging out with friends, the green-eyed jealousy monster can appear unexpectedly.

When you feel jealous, think of the happy things in your life. Count your family, friends, and pets. Don't forget pretty things in nature— like birds, butterflies, and sunny days. Think about music and books and laughter, too.

Then search through magazines to find pictures and words that show the good stuff in your life. Make a scrapbook to remind you of all your blessings. Once you realize how much you have to be happy about, the jealous feelings will start to fade away.

Somebody Needs a Helping Hand!

While you're learning to deal with jealousy, don't forget that other people cope with tough problems, too. Thinking about other people's problems can make jealousy go away.

Maybe you can make some cards and pictures to cheer up kids in the hospital. Or you could sign up as a family to serve food at a soup kitchen. Children in countries at war have scary lives. They need our love and prayers.

When we give to others, we don't have the time or energy to be jealous. It feels good making a difference in someone's life.

You Can Deal With Jealousy!

Now you have a few tricks for helping you deal with jealous feelings. You can remember that jealousy is a normal human feeling. You know that it's important to talk about it. You've learned that you can make a gratitude scrapbook and that helping out with other people's problems can take jealousy away.

If you still feel jealous way too often, ask your parents to help you think of other ways to deal with these feelings.

Praying helps, too. Ask God to guide you to be happier and more relaxed with life.

God Made You Special

Most of all, remember that God made each one of us with special skills and talents and gifts. We're all shapes and sizes. And at different times in our lives, things will feel easy or difficult.

We don't need to be jealous of other people, because God provides us with everything we need. God loves every one of us, just the way we are. And that's a great reason to feel happy and contented every day.

Molly Wigand is a writer and editor who lives in Lenexa, Kansas. She and her husband, Steve Jackson, have raised three sons who made it through jealous times and became close grown-up friends. She is the author of many children's and inspirational books, including One Caring Place publications.

R. W. Alley is the illustrator for the popular Abbey Press adult series of Elf-help books, as well as an illustrator and writer of children's books. He lives in Barrington, Rhode Island, with his wife, daughter, and son. See a wide variety of his works at: www.rwalley.com.